Chasing After
BUTTERFLIES

Chasing After

BUTTERFLIES

Sometimes it's hard to fly with wounded wings

Anna C. Bradford

authorHOUSE®

AuthorHouse™
1663 Liberty Drive
Bloomington, IN 47403
www.authorhouse.com
Phone: 1-800-839-8640

Published by AuthorHouse   06/13/2013

ISBN: 978-1-4817-6243-4 (sc)
ISBN: 978-1-4817-6242-7 (e)

Library of Congress Control Number: 2013910509

Dedication:

This book is dedicated to the lives of

Elverda Mary Chaisson, my Mother and mentor,
who worked her adult life with children.
11/14/1929-12/05/1996

William Paul Chaisson Jr. my brother who I love and miss always.
09/24/1949-07/11/1998

Joshua Jordan Bradford, my Grandson who loved to read books and sing
songs to the Lord.
03/30/2005-03/09/2007

William Paul Chaisson Sr. my Daddy who worked hard to
give us a good life.
11/26/1927

Chester Michael Chaisson my brother who made us laugh
when times were tough.

Contents

CONTENTS

Introduction

Amazing all the different desires and possessions we are inclined to pursue. Chasing after butterflies is an incredible story and a parable of life experiences and the similarities they have to a moth and a butterfly. Unbelievable journeys that take us in search of longing to be a perfect genuine monarch butterfly instead of that dull, plain and boring moth. Our longing for a colorful and meaningful life. Our yearning never to be what every one else wants us to be yet always finding ourselves in that same circumstance or situation. Throughout all of our long and tiresome searches we come to the realization that the genuine butterfly had been buried inside of us all along and longing to take to the air in flight.

We soon recognize that life is passing us by in a blink of an eye, seemingly instantaneously. We grow, look and start to feel much older. Our children begin to grow their own wings and take their own flight. As an adult, they create lives and identities of their own. Suddenly all of life's lessons and experiences are passed down to another generation and our children are now living their own lives. All that we have taught them has too soon taken flight and has produced action. Our butterflies have left the cocoon and now their lives take on spectacular but rather frightening new meanings. Our expedition of all our crooked roads stand in the hope that, some how, all of these roads will intertwine into one straight road. Our deep and dark places become light. Our split second decision suddenly become our life long consequences as well as rewards. Ultimately, we realize that our life long journey does not wait for us to make things right. In return, it gives us solid ground experiences whether good or bad. Our wisdom from our mistakes teaches us to know the difference.

We can rest knowing that all we ever have to be is what God created and desires us to be. He takes care of the rest of all the issues and problems in our lives.

In reading this book, I pray we will learn how to be content and at peace with ourselves and to release the appreciation of the life that is within us. We will live with many challenges and journeys along the way. God never promised that we would not go through battles but only said that he would be there with us in the battles and he will take us through them. We will begin to learn how to stop chasing after life long dull moths because these things have no value. Our own vain imaginations and unmeaningful particles are only dust in the wind. We will learn how to start focusing on important and essential works. Works that are contributed to the will of God. Works that become pure gold tried in the fire. Works that become precious moments that last a life time. Ultimately we will be able to live life in the most peaceful and fullest way. We will learn how to stop chasing after flesh and mothly desires that dance around in our heads. We will learn how to pursue a new and wondrous journey and start a new beginning of

"Chasing After Butterflies".

Words From The Author

My desire is for a reader to walk away from this book as a completely changed person with old things passed away and a new beginning of life as a new creation. All of our once asked questions about ourselves soon be answered. Who am I? Why am I here? What am I suppose to be doing on this earht? Time is short, precious and valuable and we are not promised tomorrow. We can take each day as a learning experience for living a fun filled life as well as a preparation for an eternal life. Finding our place in this world is not easy yet we are here to make a difference, to be an example, to be a leader and a teacher to those coming up from under us. We can spend a lot of time chasing after moths, dreams and visions that are not of God. We can chase after corruptible things instead of chasing after important, valuable and genuine butterflies. Butterflies are majestic and beautiful and represent a new creation and a new beginning. Be careful what you chase after because life has disappointments as well as accomplishments.

Ultimately, the genuine butterflies we chase after should be in compliance with the will of God. Our chasing should come from the exact guidance and direction from the Lord. God has placed a calling on every life. The ability to become a new changed creation from an old one. God gives us all kinds of chances and he wish that none should perish. Do we take these chances for granted? God has given us our own free will choices to live our lives any way that we want to. How do we choose the right way? God is always calling us with his still small voice. It is never too late until we die. The old creature nature called our flesh do have the ability to pass away and be put under subjection. All of our earthly creation and our way of living can change and become new again. We need to learn how to stop chasing after moths and start chasing after the real butterflies.

Acknowledgements

Giving glory and honor more importantly to my Lord and Savior Jesus Christ who saves me from all of my sins and place my feet upon a path of righteousness. To my husband Michael Allen Bradford Sr. whom God has placed as my soul mate to work together and fulfill the calling that God has placed on us to preach the gospel, pray for the sick, visit the prisoners, widows and orphans. I love you Mike with the special unconditional love that God has given me for you. Our three sons, Michael Allen Bradford Jr. and his wife Rebecca and all of their children. Nicholas Bradford and his wife Mary and their family and Jordan Bradford and his wife Nicole Bradford, Joshua and Jayden. I thank God every day for my families, my Mom and Dad, my sisters and brothers and all of our friends.

"Faith Without Works Is Dead"

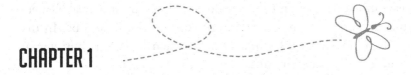

CHAPTER 1

Parable of the Moth
The Dull, Old Creature

<u>2Corinthians 5:17 Therefore if any man be in Christ he is a</u>
<u>new creature. Old things are passed away, behold, all things</u>
<u>are become new.</u>

It has always astounded me about the metamorphose of the butterfly, moth and other insects. The different stages and life span that they go through.

A cocoon is a pupa casing made by moths, caterpillars and other insects. There are exceptions but a moth can not exist unless it has been through this process. The pupa life cycle consist of four parts. The embryo, the larva, the pupa and the imago which is the last stage of development of the insect.

Wikipedia describes the differences between butterflies and moths which is the classification of the Lepidoptera. Butterflies are a natural monophyletic group often given the sub order rhopalocera

1

which includes paplionoidea. A true butterfly. A moth is Hesperidia (skippers) and hedylidar (butterfly moth). Simply speaking a moth is listed as skippers and a butterfly is listed as the true butterfly. Most moth caterpillars spin a cocoon made of silk within which they metamorphose into the pupa stage. Most butterflies on the other hand form an exposed pupa termed as chrysalis.

In the book of Mathew 6:19-20, Jesus tells us not to store up treasures on earth where moths can get to it. Don't store up treasures here on earth where moths eat them and rust destroys them and where thieves break in and steal. Store your treasures in heaven where moths and rust cannot destroy and thieves do not break in and steal. Where ever your treasure is, there the desires of your heart will also be. In the parable of the moth, earthly things can be eaten by moths but eternal things can not be eaten by moths.

Let us begin this journey where we will learn the difference between the flesh and the Spirit. The flesh is compared to a moth and is the earthly part of the man. The Spirit is compared to the genuine butterfly and is the spiritual part of the man that God created inside each of us.

Before I came to the Lord my life was as a moth. Quiet often it seemed that it was dull and boring. An everyday routine way of living where I existed but could not figure out why. Life is a process of a school and a training ground. A plan that God has ordained since before we were born. This is our temporary home and we are just passing through this journey we call life. A butterfly has such a short and special life span. All things and all people have a meaning and a purpose on this earth. In the bible the word of God says that to every thing there is a purpose under the heaven. A time to be born and a time to die, a time to plant and a time to pluck up that which was planted. A time to kill and a time to heal. A time to weep and a time to laugh. A time to mourn and a time to dance. A time to cast away stones and a time to gather stones together. A time to embrace and a time to refrain from embracing. A time to get and a time to lose. A time to keep and a time to cast away. A time to rend and a time to sew. A time to keep silence and a time to speak. A time to love and a time to hate. A time of war and a time of peace. God predetermines the events of life.

Jesus is the alpha and the omega. The first and the last. The beginning and the end. All things are created in him. He has appointed a time and a season for every thing. After Jesus died on the cross for us, he went into the depths of hell and fought and took back the keys of death from the enemy. We now have eternal life through Jesus. Our children and grandchildren have inherited that eternal life and that kingdom of God. I believe there is a greater job that children are ordained to do if they are caught up into heaven before they become adults. A job that if we had a view of the other side we could clearly see and understand. We lost our little two year old grandson Joshua, who aspirated in his sleep in 2007. I had many questions for God to answer. Questions that have not yet been answered even until this day. I grew to learn that in death there is life, a new beginning and not an end. I have seen death unite people together and I have seen death divide and destroy people. Death should never be a symbol of the end but a sure sign of the beginning. We can use death to live and bring life to others. God has given us this precious' gift. The gift of life. What we do with this special gift is our present back to God. Share the best gift of all to others. The gift of the life of Christ. The testimony of my grandson has ministered to many people and because of Joshua's passing we were able to start up a ministry under Faith Ministries, International called the "Joshua Ministry". This ministry prays and connects families who have been torn apart by their child or children passing on. We buy head stones for parents who recently experienced the death of their child. We also provide a huge yearly banquet where they can get together and visit with a support group of people who are experiencing these same difficult tragedies. We can turn death into a ministry and minister to this heavy dying world. God wants to take every bad situation and use it for his good so that his glory is manifested and established in this world and his people.

There is a time to live and a time to die on this earth. Rest in knowing that one day all of our questions will soon be answered and we will know the plans of God. Soon and very near graves will open and we will be meeting Jesus in the air where we will forever be with him. The hope that Jesus promised to every one who believes and who stand in

3

faith and wait for that glorious day. And those who have gone on before he comes will meet him in the air first.

Why are we here today? For many reasons. One is to let people know that God loves them and he has a perfect plan for their lives. You are not alone. "Fear not" I wish I had all of the answers to all of the questions but I do not. What I do have is the hope that God promised that we will be together forever one day real soon with all of our loved ones who went on before us. Jesus, which is our hope, promises us that. Outside of Jesus there is no hope for he is the hope for the world. Flesh has no hope but Spirit does.

Here is a small poem that I reflect on. I wrote it to remind myself that my life is important and we should not take it for granted. The time that God has allowed us here on this earth is so precious. We should make valuable use of it.

Seasons
Seasons change and we are another day in age
Life seems to be passing by
In a blink of an eye in becomes another day
And so we rest in him who gave his life

This is fact, God created a time and a time frame for every situation and thing. We, as individual people put on this earth by God, have special time frames to get every thing done that was required of us to do upon this earth. We are not just passing through lost in space and not knowing any direction or which road to take. God has given his plan to us and it is hidden in our hearts and in the word of God. It is up to us to search the deepest part of our heart's being and to study the word to show ourselves approved. Find the gifts within us that were deposited into us by God before creation began. Take heed now that we also have our own fleshly intentions and manly thoughts of the mind that we have to discern what is ours and what is God's placing. In the next few chapters I pray that we can begin to see exactly what is the differences between our own intentions, behaviors and our own self compares to what is the gifts, talents and intentions of God. Hopefully through this process we can begin to question our own motives, thoughts and

4

intentions. We can begin to learn how to live the authentic and actual true life that Jesus Christ paid the ultimate price for.

We have to ask ourselves do we want to live a life trying to be a genuine butterfly or a dull, unexciting moth? We strive through life trying to be some one we are not. We try to live for approval of man. Let us face reality, we can not satisfy every man. We ask ourselves also, do we want to chase after dreams to consume it upon our own flesh? Do we want to seek after our own fleshly desires? The parable of the moth's life has strongholds and bondages that can keep us from living a life of freedom and prosperity. God desires us to live the life of that true, colorful, genuine monarch butterfly. God's intensions were to never allow us to live in boredom or bondage. A bored person is one who has lost interest in life. One that somehow became uninterested in the life they are living and their surroundings. Boredom means dullness, lost luster, being annoyed over and over again, monotnous. Bored means that you are tired and fed up at what you are doing but can not seem to do anything about it. It is an empty and aimless feeling. You are aiming at nothing. Problems without solutions. A dull boring moth that flies around with nowhere to go and nothing to do. Eventually that dull moth will find itself in trouble doing things it ought not to be doing. Boredom comes from laziness and lack of self motivation. It causes you to give up on life and take you far down a vicious cycle. This cycle is almost unbreakable. Break monotny and start looking at life in another view. Suppose it was your last day on earth. Now stop and think of this just for awhile. Ask yourself what is the most important thing you need to do before you leave this earth. Now do it because we are not promised tomorrow. No one else will do it for you. Life is not a remote control. Get up and turn it yourself. With all your strength get up and move around and you will turn boredom around.

Let us begin our incredible journey and limitless flight into a long process of finding our place in this world. Our own distinguished, illustrious thumb print on this earth. Our astonishing heart reaching, soul searching experiences that will ultimately lead us into an impressive, peaceful, tranquil, prosperous and successful life. Our self controlled and disciplined life does not have to be complicated. We just need to learn how to keep specific doors closed and in some cases completely locked. Recognizing, critical consequences and to every action there is a reaction, will help you make the right decisions in life. It is often said that sometimes we have to go to the school of hard knocks and suffer heavy penalties. If we can get our flesh in line and disciplined then we can avoid some punishments before we have to pay the prices of them. If we do not get ourselves some self control then self will be out of control and it will have a costly outcome.

One has to deal with the issues of life. We all have unsettling issues in our mind and in our thoughts and even in our hearts. Some issues are not manifested and so therefore we do not realize that they are even there. Our bodies were created to have closure. We are not created to have unsettling issues dorment inside of us. These unsettled issues create feelings of despair, fears and insecurities. The flesh part which is our mind create thoughts which then create roots that lead up to strongholds. These strongholds may cripple you and hold you back into doing and living an incredible life. In the next chapter we will expose the works of our flesh and learn how we can pull down the strongholds that our flesh can create when we keep certain doors of our mind open.

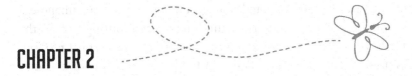

CHAPTER 2

Works Of Our Flesh And Strongholds Chasing After Moths

> *Galatians5:19-21 Now the works of the flesh are manifest, which are these : adultery fornication, uncleanness, lasciviousness, idolatry, witchcraft, hatred, variance, emulations, wrath, strife, sedition, heresies, envying, murders, drunkenness, reveling and such like of the which I tell you before, as I have also told you in the time past, that they which do such things shall not inherit the kingdom of God.*

Our flesh manifest many roots that can lead to strongholds. We can take hold of these strongholds in our lives that are holding us back from doing the things of God.

These roots that lead to strongholds confines us and can be manifested in the works of our flesh. The roots that lead to strongholds are very strong. It cripples us from walking in the Spirit of God.

Carnal, which is flesh, are thoughts and imaginations that enter our mind. They are called planted seeds. If they are not cast down or brought into captivity the seeds will take root. Seed is a fertilized and ripened egg cell of a plant, capable of sprouting to produce a new plant. Roots are the part of the plant that provides stability and nourishment for the plant. Thoughts from a seed that become plants then takes root and drop down into our hearts. For example hatred, variance, emulations, wrath, strife and bitterness are some of the roots that lead to jealousy spirit if not cast down. Hatred is contrary to the work of God. Out of the abundance of the heart the mouth speaks. We speak or act upon the seed which is the thought that was planted in our minds. The seed sprouts and becomes rooted and grounded. If you can imagine a seed germinating then you can see the long root sprouting out of the seed. Flesh, the earthly part of a person, is contrary to the spirit of God. Flesh is disobedient to the knowledge of God. The seed then grows into a stronghold. We are then walking after the lust and desires of the flesh and not after the Spirit of God. Our flesh can not please God. God has given us a free will to make choices. In one hand he gives us life and in the other hand he gives us death. God asks us which one will you choose? Physical and spiritual life comes when we are walking in his will. Physical, spiritual and eternal death comes when we are walking in our own flesh. We know that one day all will experience death unless Jesus comes before. We can experience a spiritual and eternal death if we do not take control of our flesh and if we are not in Christ. When we continue to walk in the flesh we create strongholds that hold us back from walking in the Spirit of God. Our flesh can not please God. We soon create strongholds that hold us back from walking in the Spirit of God. The commandments of God train our flesh in the way we should go. Life is in the word of God. Living without the life and the word of God causes us to live a fleshly or stronghold way of living. Let's begin to explore what are strongholds. How they develope in our lives and how can we remove and conquer them.

Strongholds

> *2Corinthians 10:4-5 For the weapons of our warfare are not carnal (flesh) but mighty through God to the pulling down of strongholds casting down imaginations and every*

high thing that exalts itself against the knowledge of God and bringing into captivity every thought to the obedience of Christ.

We all have an enemy that is out to kill, steal and destroy us. If we try to fight the enemy in the flesh we will loose. Our flesh can not fight the enemy. It is God Spirit living in us that can fight the enemy. Through God, we are mighty and can pull down the strongholds by word. Therefore bringing into captivity or in prison every thought that is contrary to God's word.

There are many kinds of strongholds that can try to keep us down. The bible calls them spirits. Understand that not all things done are spirits. In our bodies there are three areas of war going on at all time. Our flesh, the spirit of the evil one and the Spirit of God. In the next few chapters we will begin to explore all the different strongholds and their meanings and the roots that lead to all of them and finally we will learn about the Spirit of God which is the ultimate antidote for our flesh and the spirit of the enemy which is the devil.

When I first accepted Jesus Christ as my personal Lord and Savior, the Lord would speak to my spirit and I would receive revelation from him. I clearly remember one day as I was drying my hair the Lord speaking to me "Did you know that the thief came to kill, steal and destroy you. I was amazed at this true revelation for I had never heard any thing like it before. I heard him also say "Yes he stole and destroyed your marriage". The only thing that I have heard growing up and in my childhood was lies about the devil. Lies that included when it thunders the devil is beating his wife. I knew nothing of truth about the enemy that was out to destroy me. The Lord wanted me to be aware of the enemies devices but he also told me "Yes he came to kill, steal and destroy but I came to you that you will have life and have it more abundantly". A personal revelation straight from the throne room of God. Wow, I thank God for the revelation that he gave me on that morning. From that day on the Lord taught my hands to fight. By putting on his armor that we may be able to withstand the wiles of the devil and we can be protected from the enemy.

Let us begin this amazing journey together and explore all of the teachings of what our flesh does, what the enemy does and finally what the Lord God has for us. Hopefully once we are aware of the many strongholds our flesh can lead us into and where it can take us then we can choose the life that Christ has ordained for us before the foundation of the earth began.

CHAPTER 3

Jealousy
Spinning Out of Control

We all have experienced jealousy at one time or another. Some of the roots that lead to jealousy are suspicion, resentfulness, envy, bitterness, hate, strife, anger, revenge rage and murder. Webster dictionary states that suspicion is an act of suspecting, fear of something wrong, to mistrust someone or something. Suspicion is not fact. It is just a mistrust conception of someone or something. Other words for suspicion include notion, inkling, feeling, thought and misgiving.

The gift of discernment can often be working in a suspicion. God can be at some time warning you of activity that is going on and he may bring it to your attention through suspicion. Through much prayer and observation of that someone or something you can determine whether or not the suspicion is real or suspected. It may end only as a root of jealousy and prayer, binding and loosening can release it or it may be a real conception of what is really going on and you may have to further address it. Pray and ask God to expose it.

Resentfulness is another root of jealousy and is caused when resentful thoughts that are not cast down wounds our spirit. Envy is a response to a wounded spirit.

The definition of bitterness is sharp to taste, severe, painful, calamitous and is a respond to growing resent and envy. Another root of jealousy is hate. Hate means to detest, to loathe, to abhor, great dislike, to feel disgust, to abominate, to feel nausea caused by being bitter. In the bible Joseph experienced hatred from his brothers. They sold him into slavery because they were jealous of his loving relationship between him and his Father. Family hatred is nothing new. We all have a tendency to maintain a love and hate relationship with some of our siblings. One jealous member of the family comes against another. Having five other sisters growing up, we were bound to get into some spats at one time or another. Division is always lurking inside of the family. It is our responsibility to take hold of it. We need to overcome these jealousy intensions with love. My sisters and my brothers are very important to me. I grew up with a family of thirteen siblings. Growing up always around a huge family gave me a sense of security. We were never alone which, tody at times, make it difficult to be alone. We had our share of arguments but I would never want to know how it feels to be totally divided and full of hatred for one of my sisters or brothers. I will always love each of them with an unconditional kind of love.

When dealing with things of the past and accusations against us, remember in Revelations chapter ten how it states that the accuser of the brother is cast down. Our enemy is the accuser of the brother. We can not play the blame game and accuse our family for things that was done in the past. If one family member hurt another while we were young we need to let it go. When we were a child we spoke like a child but now that we are older let us put away childish things. Be kind to one another as Christ for God's sake is kind to us. Walking in love with one another no matter how hard it is. Love destroys the hatred that leads to jealousy.

Another root of the spirit of jealousy is strife. Strife is an act of striving, struggle contest, discord, conflict, quarrel of war. Acting out hurts causes competition and division.

Now anger is a violent passion, excited by real or suppose injury, resentment. It is an acting out of uncontrolling hurts rather recent or in the past.

Revenge is to take revenge for, retaliation, deliberate, getting back, infliction of injury in return for injury and being vindictive.

Rage is fury, violent rushing, frenzy, madness, physical out of control emotion.

All of these are acting out roots that lead to jealousy but the worst root of all is murder. Murder is the final act of killing a human being with premeditated malice. It is the accomplishment of what the spirit of jealousy is set to do. Other roots of jealousy include extreme competition, contention, cause division, cruelty and spitefulness. An action from anger and hatred caused by jealousy is mistreatment. Mistreatment causes hurt and harm toward others. We can sometimes have so much sorrow and pain that we take it out on other innocent people who do not deserve the mistreatement. When sorrow gets deep within our hearts sometimes we do not know how to handle the pain. We lash out at our victims who try to help. Somehow we always seem to hurt the ones we love. We have no right to hurt or harm people and anything with life and feelings. We need to keep the golden rule hidden away in our hearts. Do unto others as you would have others do unto you. At times we can not see how we are mistreating others until they give us love instead of hatred therefore giving us time to step outside of ourselves long enough to see our mistakes and mistreatments.

If we control these violent emotions before they get out of hand we can begin to practice self control. We must realize and always remember that we are complete in Jesus who is the head of all powers, principalities and rulers, spiritual wickedness in high places. Only in God we are complete and not in ourselves. If we think that our flesh is not against us we are fooling ourselves and we are in pride. Too many times the spirit of jealousy consumes a person especially a violent, domestically abused person who abuses people.

The bible says that by their fruits you shall know them. We all can discern and say that if a person has these emotions than we know that they possess evil and not good. We need to pray for the love of God to consume them. In Mathew five it speaks "Men shall revile you for my sake". If you are trying to lead a life of purity men shall revile you but great is your reward because payday is coming soon. You will be repaid by God with blessings. What the devil meant for evil God turns it for good. This earth is our temporary home. We are just passing though. We have a mansion waiting for us that Jesus is building in heaven. We need to try to treat people with kindness.

Jealousy can also be a sign of insecurities. We can get at a place in our lives where we are not secure in the life we are living. Somewhere along the road someone did us something that cause us to mistrust people. We need to stand on that solid ground and also realize that the bible says to trust no man but to put all of our trust in God. Man will always let us down. Man is not capable of being trusted. As hard as we try to unconditionally love someone we always screw up. That is why we need the precious fruit of the spirit that is a gift from God. There are nine different fruit of the Spirit. Love, Joy, Peace, Gentleness, Faithfullness, Meekness, Self Control, Temperance and Kindness. When we are walking in these fruits we are walking in Christ. When we are walking opposite to these fruits such as hatred, sadness, turmoil, roughness, unbelief, prideful, lack of control, anger and meaness then we are walking in the flesh. If we continue to walk in these bad fruits then we are under bondage and open ourselves up to strongholds. So we need to get ourselves self control but above all else, we need God to guide and take over our lives and live in our hearts.

When I had just married Mike I went through a long period in our lives where I was very jealous and insecure. When I was so young and inmature every thing seemed much more sensitive. Compounded by layers of hurt deeply rooted in my heart I can only birth this evil jealousy spirit. I needed a renewing of my mind, heart, soul and body. A cleansing that only God can do. I was spinning out of control and was consumed by an insecure life, a bitter heart full of unforgiveness and had no clue how I can get out of this terrible web that I found myself in. I created this identity that I knew nothing about nor wanted any part. I could not tear myself away from this because I was clueless at what I was going through. The love of God had been actually buried deep within me that I myself was not able to reach in and grab it. Jealousy can consume a person but love covers a multitude of sin. Jealousy crept inside of me and took root that spread deep within me. I was not at my best and was experiencing full of hatred. Jealousy is the rage of a man therefore he will not spare in the day of vengence.

The bible speaks that a jealous husband will have fury and show no mercy when he takes revenge. Jealousy shows no partiality and is weak to all gender. Our flesh would rather at times show hatred, bitterness and strife instead of love hugs and kisses. Opening a door to the spirit of jealousy is dangerous. We can keep that door shut by casting down sudden thoughts, feelings and fleshly emotions that causes jealousy to rise up. Cast it down while it is just a thought then it will not have any feelings to build upon. Be sensitive and do not give reason for place of jealousy. Honor your spouse and do not open any door even if they have given you reason to be jealous. Communicate with your spouse. Let them know how you feel in all situations. Quiet discussions and not angry arguments have solved many jealousy problems. A soft answers turns away wrath. Pray and go to God with the situation and watch him take care of it all. God has proven that he is for our marriages. He is on our side when we try to work things out. What God has joined together let no man bring us under.

Saul hated David but David did not allow the hatred to get into his heart. David never took revenge even when he could have easily killed Saul. Instead he cut off a piece of his garment to prove to Saul that he was close enough to harm him but chose not to. God awarded David the kingship and the nation at the age of thirty.

Jealousy is hereditary. Children will listen at their Mom or Dad criticize a person and speak evil against that person. They will criticize that same perso. They will speak and feel the same way that their parents spoke and felt of them. If they were brought up to speak evil against a person they will hate that person. The seed of bitterness becomes rooted and grounded and they begin to act out what was planted deep in their hearts at an early age. Jesus never seeked revenge. He asked the Father to forgive them for they know not what they are doing. He traded jealousy and hatred for love and salvation. The antidote for jealousy is forgiveness. When God forgives us he throws it into the sea of forgetfulness. He never picks it back up. He will never say "oh by the way". God throws it as far as the east is from the west.

We are to strive to teach love instead of hatred. Life is too short to live in jealousy or revenge. We loosen the chains that bind us up when we release the jealousy. Forgiving a person frees us up more than the person needing the forgiveness. It is given to us to heal all of wounds that we were tormented by. It delivers our heart from life long bondages that keep us in the darkness.

> *Numbers 5:14 And the spirit of jealousy come upon him, and he be jealous of his wife, and she be defiled: or if the spirit of jealousy come upon him, and he be jealous of his wife, and she be not defiled:*
> *Numbers 5:30*
>
> *Or when the spirit of jealousy cometh upon him, and he be jealous over his wife, and shall set the woman before the LORD, and the priest shall execute upon her all this law.*
> *Love 1Cor. 13:4-8*
>
> *Love sufferes long and is kind. Love envies not. Love vaunts not itself, is not puffed up. Does not behave itself unseemly. Seeks not her own, is not easily provoked, thinks no evil. Rejoice not in iniquity but rejoice in the truth. Bears all things, believes all things, hopes all things, endures all things. Love never fails, but whether there be prophecies, they shall fail. Whether there be tongues, they shall cease, Whether there be knowledge it shall vanish away.*

CHAPTER 4

Fear
Afraid of Taking Flight?

It has been often said that there is nothing to fear but fear itself. Fear is a real feeling. Understanding the roots that lead to the spirit of fear can release you from the grip that fear has upon you. Some of the roots include anxiety. Anxiety is a displeasing feeling of fear and concern. A state of uneasiness and apprehension. Throughout my life I have experienced the very prescense of fear. Anxiety causes a flutter in your heart. Many people go through their whole lives living with anxiety. Some know why while others are clueless as to why they always feel anxious. It is very important to understand why you are feeling anxious. Search your heart if it has not yet surfaced. If you know why you are being anxious, cry it out. Release it out of you. Pray and ask God to deliver you. Cry it out to Jesus.

> *Psalm 46:1-5 God is our refuge and strength, a very present help in trouble. Therefore will not we fear, though the earth be removed, and though the mountains be carried into the midst of the sea. Though the waters there of roar and*

be troubled, though the mountains shake with the swelling thereof, there is a river the streams whereof shall make glad the city of God, the holy place of the tabernacles of the most high. God is in the midst of her she shall not be moved. God shall help her and at the break of dawn.

Dismay means to break down the courage of completely, as by sudden danger or trouble, dishearten thoroughly to cause someone to feel discouraged or disappointed. Throughout our lives we all have had people that broke down our courage and has caused us to be discouraged or disappointed. We should not let man dictate how we are going to feel. The joy of the Lord is our strength. The world did not give us joy so the world definitely can not take it away from us.

Another root of fear is terror. Terror is intense, sharp, overmastering fear. To be frantic with terror. Instance or cause of intense fear or anxiety, quality of causing terror to be a terror to evildoers. One that instills intense fear. Dogs can instill intense fear in me. When I was a young girl I was attacked by a dog. The dog continued to bite me all the way home. This experience can put a fear in anyone. As I grew older fear of dogs stayed in me. One day I was riding my bike when I got older and a huge dog jumped a ditch and headed right in the path of my bike. Fear gripped me and I could sense the terror go down my spine. It would take God's delivering power to get me out of this situation. I could clearly remember thinking in my mind that this dog is going to put me in the hospital with bite marks all over my body. I immediately started to pray in the Spirit because my words in my thought process were not coming. By the grace of God the dog made a complete oppposite turn in the other direction. I had just witnessed a miracle and a deliverance from fear at the same time. There are times in my life that fear does try to come back upon me again but I remember what God had done and he is the same yesterday, today and forever.

The root panic is a sudden overpowering terror, often affecting many people at once. Panic attacks sometimes overpowers a person leaving them cripple to move or speak or function in an ordinary way. On 911 every one was hit with sudden panic of fear. Terrorist cause terror and pain to their victims. They keep their victims in their dominating control. It is very important not to allow terrorist to control you. Jesus said that mens hearts will give out because of fear. It will make a body ill. Panic attacks manifest itself in many people.

Tension means the act of stretching or straining mental or emotional strain, intense, suppressed suspense, anxiety or excitement. A strained relationship between individuals, groups and nations etc. When you are going through a strained relationship such as a difficult time in your marriage it can set off plenty of tension. Also when you are denying something that has been done to you and you have not dealt with it you will not be able to escape tension. It is a root of fear caused by some one or something that needs to be dealt with.

Defeat means to win victory over, beat, to prevent success of, to overcome in a contest. Your enemy wants victory over you. He does not want you to succeed. If we do not give up we can win the battle and be victorious.

We can experience a healthy fear that comes from God. An alarm that goes off in our minds reminding us that danger is near. An example is that our minds will warn us if we are near a fire not to get too close. This type of fear is discernment from God. Discernment is one of the many ministry gifts that God has given us. It allows us to distinguish good from evil. Fear can be also an alarm caused by our adversary (the enemy). Fear grows in our body when there are hidden seeds of thoughts. Unknown secrets of the heart that needs to be exposed. Fear is exposed by discussing or acknowledging that fear is near. A person can sometimes not know that there are seeds of fear hiding in their thoughts and minds. It could have been because they were too young to remember what had happened. They might not have remembered that someone did something to them at a very early age and it was buried deep inside of their heart. Hidden fears are fears that have been hidden in the heart for long periods of time. Fears that grew and took root from hurts that were not dealt with or hurts that people do not want to deal with. Our concious mind is in fear of exposing subconcious thoughts.

If we do not address the roots that lead to fear then we will never totally remove fear from us.

The bible states that God has not given us a spirit of fear but he gave us power, love and a sound mind.

Fear is a phobea and there are many kinds of phobeas.

Fear of the unknown is a fear of not knowing what is going to happen. It often occurs when we are facing changes in our lives. Life turns in another direction. This fear creates a mixture of lonliness and heaviness. Being a creature of schedule and routine, when I was taken out of the ordinary and into the uncommon then fear would want to dominate. My reactions would be totally unacceptable to this. I am not always willing to accept the unknown. Not knowing what will happen or what situation will take place can be difficult to acknowledge. Living the life of a missionary changed me to accept the unknown. We live and walk by faith and the will of God. I find myself feeling less anxious. We should prepare ourselves to be creatures of change because life has changes and leads us into many different directions. We should never be satisfied and be comfortable in one place. We will always go through mountains and valleys and many rough and crooked roads. We should teach ourselves to be contented at whatever state we find ourselves in.

Fear of death is a constant worrying that you, your family or soemone you love is going to die. Worrying is that root of fear. Remember Jesus came to earth to pay the price of death so that we can live eternally.

Another sign of fear is being alone or lonliness. In this fear you can never stay alone because it is too scary. Roots of tension take hold. Other phobeas such as fear of insect, snake or rodent phobeas are fears that give off lots of stress. Other signs of fear include fear of people or not able to get out of your house. The majority of these roots that lead to fear start when we are children and follow us all of our lives. Fear will never go away if you do not deal with it. We have to face our fear and bring it to the surface. Search your heart to find out why is it that you are afaid of something. My weakness to mice stems from when I was a child I went into the barn to feed the horses. As I opened the corn barrel I was so startled when a colony of mice squirmed their way out. It terrified me to the point that I was petrified. That seed of fear planted itself deep within my being. Not dealing with this root began a long life of fear of mice. Test yourself at what fears you the most. Name one of your fears out loud. Try and remember when you have encountered this thing that created fear in you. Now deal with the roots that lead to the fear you are encountering. If you are experiencing panic attacks then cry it out and do not hold in tears. Many times we have not cried for a very long time therefore stifling so much fear inside of us. These fears can suffocate us and make us unable to breathe properly. Tears are a healing of the heart. God created tears to melt away the problems in the heart like a lighted candle melts away the wax. More importantly we need to pray for faith. Faith is the opposite of fear. If you are afraid of being alone then you need to have faith in knowing that God is going to keep you safe and he will never leave you or forsake you. We not only can say it but we also have to speak it out loud and get it down in our hearts. Out of the abundance of the heart the mouth does speak. What is in the heart will manifest itself and you will speak or act it out. Every thing that is hidden will be revealed. Uneasy feelings of fear and other strongholds has to surface because the body was never intended to be in such anxieties due to strongholds. Standing on the word of God is the healing of any fear. What so ever we bind on earth is bound (by the will of the Father) in heaven from our Father and what so ever you loosen (by the will of the Father) on earth is loosen by our Father. We have that same freedom given to us. We have all power and authority from Jesus to free ourselves and any other person from strongholds that are leading us away from God and from true selves. Binding fear and loosening faith always works. Jesus said what so ever you ask the Father in my name (Jesus) he will do.

Another kind of fear is fear of insanity. Sometimes the enemy plays tricks with our minds and make us think that we are going crazy and that we will not make it. The root of defeat has grown in us. Our minds can not comprehend victory over things or a person. We become weak minded. Our minds become unstable and include thoughts of defeat which produces a feeling of hopelessness or death. This is where the enemy wants to keep you and to prevent you from being successful and an overcomer. God says that we are complete in him who is the head of all powers and principalities and ruler of darkness. Who is the ruler of darkness? The enemy, the devil himself.

Other signs of fear include alarms caused by our adversary the devil because God did not give us the spirit of fear. Unresolved roots that lead to fear can produce many scary thoughts. Fear also produces terror which is a frightening feeling encountered from an experience. Stress and anxiety is also a root of fear that causes body tension and sometimes physical illnesses. Anxiety causes panic attacks. Tension and worrying comes out of fear also. Our minds have the tendency to worry about things we have no control over. Our thoughts can literally scare us to death. Fear of man or people and other fears such as opposition keeps us in bondage to the fear. Fear of the future or fear of the unknown is a fear that we have when we are not aware of what is going to happen in the near or far future. Fear that the outcome will not turn out good. A negative thought at all times. Fear of speaking is not being able to speak in front of people. Fear of the night keeps us up at night and will not allow us to get the proper rest we need.

The first sign of fear began when sin came into the world.

Genesis 3:10 And he said I heard thy voice in the garden and I was afraid because I was naked and I hid myself. Fear and shame was never noticeable until sin came in by the serpent deceiving Adam and Eve. They became frightened when they knew they were naked and had not experienced good from evil before. The tree of knowledge between good and evil was simply that. If we eat of the tree of knowledge between good and evil we will know the differece between good and evil. God protected Adam and Eve from evil until they ate of the fruit and sin came in. They had no fear or worries because the planting of the seed that led to the stronghold of fear had not been planted in the thoughts and minds of Adam and Eve therefore fear was nowhere to be found. The roots of fear were not growing inside of them because there was no imagination or high thoughts that exalted itself against the knowledge of God. They believed and walked with God in the cool of the day. They never doubted or experienced hatred, strife or sin because sin was nowhere to be found. It had not been born into the world yet. When Adam and Eve ate of the forbidden fruit they entered into a spiritual battle between good and evil, the battle between God and the devil. They had been innocent to evil and only experienced the goodness and relationship of God. Before this God kept his battles with the devil to himself. His intensions were never to include us into his conflict. By disobedience we included our ownselves. We opened that door by eating that forbidden fruit. They were suddenly introduced to evil. They realized their nakedness and was ashamed. They were afraid because they were naked. Every thing opposite of good had been birthed that day. Man would never be the same. Our innocence was tainted on that day. Our advisary the devil had a foot hole in the door of our minds. The door to our minds, emotions and feelings had been swung wide open and the seeds that were planted from the disobedience of Adam and Eve made roots. These roots turned into strongholds and the battle between the enemy and our soul began. The enemy birthed sin into our carnal flesh. Suddenly Adam and Eve found themselves needing God to intervein on their behalf. Today we find ourselves needing God to intervein on our behalf also.

For the weapons of our warfare are not carnal but mighty through God to the pulling down of strongholds casting down imaginations and every high thing that exalts itself against the knowledge of God and bringing into captivity every thought to the obedience of Christ. Our flesh can not fight the enemy. Though God we are mighty and can pull down the strongholds by casting down every vain imagination and every thought against God and his word. Therefore bringing into captivity or in prison every thought that is contrary to God's word.

The antidote for fear is faith. Fight fear with faith believing that the word of God wll not come back void but it does what it was sent out to do. Quote the word and stand on it.

God did not give us a spirit of fear but he gave us the power when he sent his son Jesus to die on the cross for us. He gave us power when his son left this earth to build a new Jerusalem for us and left us the Holy Spirit. By the trinity we are able to overcome fear. Our faith is the opposite of the fear. We must overcome fear by our faith.

When fear takes grip of you call out to Jesus.

2Timothy 1:7 For God has not given us the spirit of fear but of power, and of love and of a sound mind.

CHAPTER 5

Whoredom
Bounded And Flightless

The manifested works of our flesh is adultry, fornication, uncleanness and many other fleshly desires. If not casted down they become strongholds in our lives. One of the stronghold that our flesh lead us into is the spirit of whoredom. Some of the roots that lead to whoredom are fornication, adultry, sexual sins, harlotry, prostitution, self exaltation and idolatry which is spiritual adultry. The definition of whoredom is the practice of whoring, prostitution, faithless, unworthy or idolatrous practices or pursuits. Fornication means consensual sexual intercourse between two persons who are not married to each other. Adultry is voluntary sexual intercourse between a married man and someone other than his wife or between a married woman and someone other than her husband. It is an unfaithful act committed against a marriage. God created sex for our pleasure. God also set limits for our protection on how sex should be enjoyed. If we go outside of those limits we cross the boundary of and enter into sexual sin. The old sayings such as "Why buy the cow when you can get the milk free" or "Try it before you buy it" has bombarted our thoughts and establishes the way some of us live today. Everywhere we turn these days there are couples engaging in premarital and extra marital sex. We can not turn the television on without it showing or suggesting sex. This fills our minds up with thoughts to go ahead and have an extra marital affair or go ahead and have sex with your boyfriend. As Christian we have a moral obligation not to do this. When we live with Christ we have certain guidelines to follow. Certain boundaries that can not be crossed. The seventh commandment God instructs us not to commit adultry and have sex with any one else except our partner and mate. God forbids sex outside of marriage for many reasons. God created Adam and Eve and the two became one. It is God's will that two people come together as one but not outside of the marriage. Outside of the marriage sex is flesh. Two people uniting together inside of a marriage releases a spiritual union. Two people respecting one another and saving each other for a pleasurable time and a spiritual time. If we wait we encounter a spiritual blessing from God. If we live in the carnal and fleshly nature and go after sex outside of the marriage we seek to gratify pleasing our own flesh. If we seek to please our own flesh than we are not able to please God. It becomes sin and we become crushed and weighed down from our sin. Our flesh rises up and our spiritual being grow weak. Ultimately we become led by our own fleshly desires and not by the will of God. Sin leads to sin and the end of sin is death. Our sinful nature is destroyed by our own doings. Sin is a curse place upon us by our own fleshly desires or by the enemy. The tempter paint such a beautiful picture. Speaking to your mind words like this person cares for you more than your own husband or wife. This person acknowledges you and wants to spend more time with you than your husband or wife. Divided words that end you up in divorce. Jesus saids the guidelines for marriage and divorce in the book of Mark chapter 10:6-12 Jesus states "But from the beginning of the creation God made them male and female. For this cause shall a man leave his Father and Mother and cleave to his wife and they two shall become one flesh so then they are no more two but one flesh. What therefore God hath joined together let no man put asunder. He goes on to say in verse eleven and twelve "Whosoever shall put away his wife and marry another, commites adultery against her. And if a woman put away her husband, and be married to another, she committs adultery. In 1Corinthians 7:10-16 we find the principles for the married believer. This is for the Christians who are married. And unto the married I command yet not I but the Lord. Let not the wife depart from her husband. But and if she depart, let her remain unmarried, or be reconciled to her husband and let not the husband put away his wife. Paul goes on to say that it is him who speaks that if a wife has a husband who is an unbeliever and if he be pleased to dwell with her, let her not leave him. For the unbelieving husband is sanctified by the wife. But if the unbelieving depart let him depart. A brother or a sister is not under bondage in such cases but God hath called us to peace. It is good for a man not to touch a woman. Nevertheless, to avoid fornication let every man have his own wife and let every woman have her own husband. Let the husband render unto the wife due benevolence (affection) and likewise also the wife unto the husband. The priciples for the unmarried and widows is if they cannot contain let them marry for it is better to marry than to burn. The principle for the remarriage is that the wife is bound by the law as long as her husband lives but if her husband be dead, she is at liberty to be married to whom she will, only in the Lord. This means to stay within the guidelines of a life with having the Lord in control of your life. I married my high school sweetheart. We made many mistakes. I had left my first love, Jesus and the path that God had me on. I rebelled against my parents and left home to be with Mike. He was so adventuous and I loved it. Mike was my first and we did have sex outside of the marriage. I did get pregnant for my oldest child one month after I graduated from high school. When I returned for my graduation ceremony I was three months pregnant. I was pressured in it by my own weak mindness. I did not take a stand in my moral values. We did eventually marry soon after my graduation ceremony but Mike's respect for me had been jeopardized. This caused him to think less of me morally. I was not a perfect example to him therefore I was not able to teach him any values of God at that time. Actually it had become my downfall of loosing my own identity. I was raised a catholic girl, living out in the country, the only house on the street. I had a life, by God, tucked far away from society and the cruel world that I was innocent to. Sheltered and naive to the evil things of the world. Cocooned in my own innocence, my freedom from sin, moral wrong and free from all guilt. I hung around a small group of friends and the world called us "The L7 group"(Square). I had not heard of the word pot until I met Mike. I had not been taught how to be strong minded. I had no will to say no when I needed to. Having the tendency to always see the good in everyone because my Dad tried to shelter me from all of the bad things that would try to come my way. Soon I found myself living the life style that he so desperately tried to shelter and protect me from.

Some of the blessings that we encounter when we do not take heed to sin is that we will live a healthier life mentally, spiritually and physically. When we make the choice to be faithful to our spouse then we are walking in the Spirit of God. This is where God wants us to stay. We avoid sexually transmitted diseases. We avoid untimely and unplanned pregnancies. We avoid excessive baggage of guilt and shame that linger in our minds. If we put our spouse before our own feelings we honor and respect them. We honor and repect the other couple also if we choose not to have a sexual relationship with their spouse. There are so many consequences of sin. Divorce is one of the main consequences. God hates divorce. Sometimes a marriage can not hold up when adultry had been performed. Although there can be forgiveness in a relationship we may never be able to forget. It may take a long time for a person to heal when someone has proven disloyalty to them. Trust has to be earned again and sometimes we can not get it back because of fear and insecurities.

Our job is to shine our light into a dying world. In order for us to do that we have got to be followers of Christ and become an example of how to live in freedom. We are not able to attract the world and shine our light if we live in total darkness.

When we choose to live in sexual immorality we settle for less than what God has for us and our partner.

If we choose to have sex before marriage or have an extra marital relationship we need to acknowledge this warning sign in our own spiritual condition. We should strive for God's perfect will and not settle for less.

Let's face it. Life is tough and hard. Sometimes we try to live a Godly life and we struggle with it. One day we are living one way and the next we realize that the road we were going down was not the road God intended for us.

We suddenly realize we veered off that straight and narrow road and had been confused and led by temptation.

The bible speaks a lot about temptation. God will not suffer us to be tempted more than we can stand. He will always make a way out of temptation.

No wrong has never been right. We need to live with integrity and not be carried away from our own lust. Temptation starts in our flesh then in our soul and ends up in our spirit. The first temptation was in the garden of Eden when Adam and Eve was tempted by the serpent. Bowing down to temptation has drastic consequences as sin came into the world when Eve ate of the fruit and gave some to her husband. It was not the fruit they ate that made it wrong but it was the forbidden fruit that God told them not to eat. Therefore the door was open because of the disobedience. Every human being is tempted by his own lust. Our flesh is enemies to God and certainly the devil himself is an enemy to God. We are drawn away by the temptation of the lust and evil in our own heart. Why are we tempted? Because the devil hates us and wants us seperated from our creator and maker. When we are allured into doing something we know is wrong we can not see the final picture of the whole idea behind it. At times it looks like there is nothing wrong with what we are doing then the consequences slap us in the face. We become aware of the purpose of what the temptation was all about. Created to destroy us, temptation does just that. We fall right into the trap that was laid out for us. God wants us to avoid all hurts to ourselves and others by keeping the doors of temptation shut, locked and bolted.

If we have led an adulturous life and have been living in the lust thereof John 8:11 tells us to go and sin no more.

Hypothetically speaking, your in love with a person that is not available, a forbidden love. You fight the temptations and the thoughts of the mind. You are constantly at war with this and you really love this person with all of your heart, mind and being. You cry out daily because you want this person so much to be a part of your life. You know it is wrong but your flesh is really gaining power over your Spirit. When you try to talk yourself out of loving this person, it does not work and at times it seems as if it is getting even stronger and more intense. You think you have it beat then you are knocked down again when you hear the person's name. There is a recurring incident like a phone call or you see this person again. All of these emotions start to stir up again. This unforbidden love issue will not go away even though you tried to fight it with all of your power. At times it seems so right but then you go back to the word of God and his word proves that it is wrong. At times you feel it is too valuable to place in God's hands and have his will be done with it. We hold on to issues that are so dear to our hearts. It becomes our life line. It guides and leads us. It controls our heart. What we are experiencing is an emotional attachment. Once we attach ourselves to someone or something there has to be a detachment. We have to clip those attachments and that is not so easy to do. We have given authority to our flesh.

Guard your heart with all diligence because out of it flows the issues of life. Your love isssue is flowing and is living but is it right? Is it the issue of love that God gave you or is it your own will? The issues of life, love and the pursuit of happiness always manifests itself when it is not dealt with. The issues of the heart needs to be acknowledged, exposed and discussed in order to resolve and find closure.

Acknowledge: Acknowledge the truth and do not hide it. Every thing hidden will be revealed. Every isssue has to come up to surface. Speak the truth. Yes I love this person. I will always love this person. I love this person with all of my heart, mind, and flesh. This person is very dear to me and maybe one day we will be together according to the plan of God and only if it is the plan of God. Acknowledge your feelings and do not hide anything. It will not go away if you bury your head in the sand sort of speak.

Expose: Confessing the truth exposes the issue and reveals it. Exposing defines it whether it is wrong or right. Exposing the issue causes us to ask questions. Is this love leading me down another path? Will this love lead me toward or away from God? Answer all the questions that you will have truthfully.

Resolve: Does this love break any of God's commandments? Does it go against the word of God?

Closure: What is the solution to this problem? In order to find closure to this heart felt issue we need to come to the conclusion that by the word of God we can desolve the things that are not of God. Although this is easier said than done we still need to do what is right according to the word of God. Our flesh will not want this process and will fight it at all times. Our flesh is an enemy to God.

But there is peace in overcoming these issues. When we resolve these issues in our mind, because it starts by a thought in the mind, then we can resolve it in our heart. Fix the mind and you will fix the heart and ultimately you will fix what the mouth speaks. We fix this by the commandments and the word of God. Out of the abundance of the heart the mouth does speak. When we find the solution then it is our choice to walk it out. Remember God spoke life in one hand and desth in the other but he goes on to tell us which one to choose. Choose life! Physical and Eternal life is when we are walking in the Spirit. If we walk in the Spirit you shall not fulfill the lust of the flesh. The flesh will fight the word of God every time but as hard as it is we need to walk in the Spirit of God by following his ways. When we do this we win the war of the flesh. The enemy wants us to walk in the flesh because this is where he wins every time. Walking in our flesh causes confusion in the mind and the enemy can gain control over our thoughts and over our flesh. Our flesh can not win the battle. We need the Spirit of God to win not only this battle but to win every war.

CHAPTER 6

Religion
Reality Flightless

God is looking for one pure at heart. One that will say "Here I am Lord Send Me, Use Me" One that no matter what comes at them, they will not bow down. They will not give up and throw in the towel. One that God wants to use to cry out for the people of the land. One that has the pure discernment and the genuine heart of God. One that hates sin and loves truth and honesty and obedience. God wants to heal our land from evil and demonic forces but there is not one true person he can find or is there? Sin and lawlessness continues and the devil walks around as a lion seeking to eat you up but God is seeking someone righteous and anti religious. Someone not wearing a mask nor a fake, not religious people. If he could just find that one person then so much of the kingdom of God will be impacted. So many of Gods people have been martyred, pressed down, crushed, packed down, trodden, replaced and compacted. It is time for us to rise up and take the place that God has called us to. Remove the mask that hides who we truly are and not just remove it but replace it with the factual, existent person that God wants us to be and that he created us to be.

31

Our flesh can cause us to live a false life. One thought, if not casted down, can lead us down a road that seems right but yet the end result is death and destruction.

If we are not careful of the things of the flesh our flesh can bring us into a religious way of living. We soon loose our identity and start to live a life that is not intended for us.

Some of the roots that lead to a religious spirit is traditions of man, false religion, false teaching, anti semitism, racism, prejudice, animism-idolatry-newage-pagen-heathen-worship of trees, gardens, nature worship, sun worship, worshiping wood and stone.

God is a Spirit and they that worship him must worship him in Spirit and truth. The Spirit of God is in our heart when we have accepted Jesus Christ as our personal savior. To get to the Father we must go though the son because the Father, Son and Holy Spirit are one. God sent his only son into the world (God in the flesh). Jesus died for our sins so that we can be forgiven and reconciled back to God. He is the only way, the truth and the light and no man can come to the Father except by him. When we try to come to God any other way except through Jesus Christ we are building a religious way of living instead of a relationship with God.

Living a religious life means that we are not having a personal relationship with God. We are not in religion when we have a personal relationship with God. If we take our eyes off of Jesus and place it on something or someone else steers us into another direction. We can start to live an idolatrous life. Seek first the kingdom of God and his righteousness and everything else will follow. According to Wikipedia, the free encyclopedia, Religion is quoted as an organized collection of beliefs, cultural systems and world views that relate humanity to the supernatural, to spirituality and sometimes to moral values. Many religions have narratives, symbols and sacred histories that are intended to create meaning to life or traditionally to explain the origin of life or the universe. From the beliefs about the cosmos and human nature they tend to derive morality, ethics, religious laws or a preferred lifestyle. There is said to be over 4,200 religions in the world. Practices of religion mawy include rituals, sermons, commemoration or veneration of a deity, gods, or goddesses, sacrifices, festivals, feasts, trance, initiations, funerary services, meditation, prayer, music, art, dance, public service or other aspects of human culture. Religion may also contain mythology. In 2012 a global poll reports that 59% of the world's population is religious, 23% are not religious and 13% are atheists.

We must be excellent to what is good and innocent to evil. If your religion causes you to hate your brother then you need to get out of that religion. God is Love. Judgement belongs to God. We should never harm another soul just for the sake of their beliefs.

We can go all over and confess many things but when we confess that Jesus is Lord it stirs up many devils. You can speak any name and scream it out at the top of your lungs. You might not get any response but speak the name of Jesus and see if you will not have someone ask you "Why are you cramming religion down our throats"? Speak the name of Jesus and see if you will be looked upon as a lunetic or some crazy person. Something about the name of Jesus that causes a stir in the Spirit of man. Sin can not abound when Jesus is around. Jesus shines his light upon you. He is the light of the world, a city on a hill. The name of Jesus is either the most loved name that exist or the most hated name, depending on which side you are on.

CHAPTER 7

Jezebel
Broken Wings

The majority of people are innocent of evil and have no spiritual or history knowledge of the Jezebel spirit. The Jezebel spirit is one of the evil spirits that belong to satins demonic forces. Some of its cultures are Mother-child related, cult of Simiramis-Tammuz which entered other cultures as Ashtoreth-Baal, Aphrodite- Eros, Venus- Cupid and Madonna-child. The roots to Jezebel are false prophetess, false teachings, dominating and controlling, religious and traditional, seducing and she is the mother of all harlots. Other roots consist of fornication, sexual immorality, idolatry, self exultation and arrogance.

Where I grew up, which is about sixty miles south of New Orleans, Louisiana, the city loves its parades and they actually spread to all of the surrounding cities now. Every year in February, which is six weeks before Easter, carnival comes around and people are voted in as queen, king, dukes and maidens. Each float crew creates their own floats. The main day is called "Fat Tuesday". This is the day before ash Wednesday which is a religious holiday. I believe every one in the United

States has heard of "Mardi Gras". One of the groups name is Aphrodite Crew. This crew consist of only women. This falls right into the Jezebel rooted culture.

History and the bible tells us that the fountainhead of idolatry, (Jezebel) is the mother of harlots and abominations of the earth. The harlot has killed many of Gods saints and Christian martyrs throughout the ages and will do so again during the tribulation. In revelation of the bible Christ called the great harlot Jezebel, self proclaimed prophetess, leading the church into false doctrine, idolatry, and immorality just as old testament jezebel had done to Israel in 1king 16 and 2king 9.

Repeated warnings and chastisements were given to her by the Lord.

In Revelation 2: 18 The church of Thyatira is located 20 miles south east of Pergamos, the home town of Lydia, Paul's first convert in Macedonia. Fire and brass is Christ's promise to judge the false teachers of this church. This city was controlled by a female-dominated by a dye and cloth industry.

In Revelation, the harlot (Jezebel) has been described as sitting on many waters on the beast and on seven mountains. Here the waters are identified as people and multitude, nations and tongues, indicating the worldwide influence and authority of the harlot. In verse 18 of chapter 17 she is described as the great city, which reigns over the kings of the earth referred probably to a world wide idolatrous pagan system centered at Rome toward the end of the tribulation period, however, the ten kings (verse 12) will destroy the harlot system chapter 18:6-24. They will do this as Gods will and turn their total devotion and worship to the beast itself, (13:12, 17:13, Dan. 11:36-39).

Believers must be separated to the harlot system, or else they may be found to share in her sins and therefore receive part of her judgment. The double judgment emphasizes full punishment for her sins. That she calls herself a queen and no widow shows her arrogant, self confidence. She sees herself as beyond possibilities of personal sorrow.

35

God, at last, judges the Babylon system for its treatment of God's people particularly those who are martyred during the tribulation.

Jezebel refused to repent therefore would be judged along with her children (or disciples). Everyone who follows her ways will be destroyed. 1king 21:25 And of Jezebel also spoke the Lord saying dogs shall eat Jezebel.

Since Ahab humbled himself to the Lord evil was put on his sons days and not in his days. Deuteronomy 7:3 says that we shall not make marriages with them. In the old testament they threw Jezebel down and the horse trod under her.

But a Godly remnant refused to accept these deep teachings or depths of satin. In the book of Romans we are to be excellent at what is good and innocent of evil. To hold fast to what is good and reject evil.

Ahab married Jezebel, the daughter of Ethbaal, king of Ionians and went and served Baal and worshipped him. Jezebel's name means "Where is the prince"? (Baal). Ahab's reign was to bring Israel to its spiritual depths. Ahab was a passive man and let Jezebel's power rule him.

In 1King he reared up an altar for Baal in the house of Baal which he had built in Samaria. Ahab made a wooden image (grove) and Ahab did more to provoke the Lord God of Israel to anger than all the kings of Israel that were before him. He was a chief deity of ancient Canaan. The son of El. Baal was both a heroic figure, as a storm god, and a fertility deity who was worshiped in many cult centers under various forms. Judges 12 tells us that the children of Israel forsook the Lord, and served Baal and Ashtoreth (Canaanite Goddesses). God brought them out of the Land of Egypt, and they followed other gods of the people that were around them, and provoked the Lord to anger. When the Lord used Moses to set his people free, he parted the Red Sea so that they can live in a land flowing with milk and honey. When Moses was upon the mountain receiving words and instructions from the Lord the children of Israel, along with Aaron, was making a golden calf which were to be used for them as their false god. The Lord was angry with the people and

Moses struck down the ten commandments that God gave him and the people to live by. While he had been in the mountains they were sining and worshiping the golden calf.

A list of other cult centers under various forms are Baalim (plural of Baal). Ashtoreth (or Ashtoreth 1king 11:5). This was a goddess of erotic love and war. She also was known as Ishtar or Astarte. Ishtar or Astarte entered the Mediterranean world under the name of Astarte, and their practices became associated with the Greek goddess of love, Aphrodite. She was called Atargatis at Ashkelon. The Canaanite worship rites were carried out not only in temples but on every high hill and under every green tree according to 2kings 17:10, 11.

Jezebel's rites consisted of frenzied dances, cult, prostitution, (both male and female), and at times human sacrifices as in Jeremiah 19:5-7 with 2king 23:10, Jeremiah 7:30-32 and 32:30-35,

Jezebel thrives on being the number one in control and dominates people into standing on her side. Consisting of many spirits into one stronghold. Seducing, manipulating, jealousy, whoredom and many other roots and spirits. She will even bring your own husband or wife into her net. That spirit will try to prove that it can have any one. But by the blood of Jesus Christ, it is bounded and cast away into the pit of hell where it belongs.

So the very existence of Mardi Gras is an abomination to the Lord if you are entering and partaking into the rituals and the statues of idoltrous affairs. You are receiving and bowing down to evil rituals that the Lord is against. We are merely bringing back to life, each time we celebrate, the greek mytholocism that the Lord hates.

CHAPTER 8

Lying
Traveling By Truth

Psalm 119:163, Prov. 12:19, 20, 22 Ephes. 4:25

Roots:

Sedition—Conduct or language inciting rebellion against the authority of a state. A revolt or an incitement to revolt against established authority, usually in the form of treason or defamation against government.

Usually protected by "Free Speech" so prosecution is very rare. It is a crime in the United States which outlaws the advocating, the overthrow of the federal government by force. Galatian 5:20, Ezek. 4:15

This root is one of the works of the flesh listed in Galatians.

Heresies-Belief of opinion contrary to orthodox religion (especially Christian) doctrine. Opinion profoundly at odds with what is generally accepted.

2Peter2:1-2 But there were false prophets also among the people even as there shall be false teachers among you who privily shall bring in damnable heresies even denying the Lord that brought them, and bring upon themselves swift destruction. And many shall follow their pernicious ways by reason of whom the way of truth shall be evil spoken of.

Another root of the lying spirit is Deceit, the action or practice of deceiving someone by concealing or misprepresenting the truth. A dishonest act or statement. Prov. 12:19

2Peter 2:10-22 describes false teachers. They walk after the flesh in the lust of uncleanness.

Synonyms- deception, fraud, cheat, trickery, trick, guile.

We have a choice to walk either in a lying spirit of in the Spirit of Truth. Spirit of Truth is the antidote for the lying spirit. John16:13 Howbeit when he, the Spirit of Truth is come, he will guide you into all truth for he shall not speak of himself but whatsoever he shall hear that shall he speak and he will show you things to come. The Spirit of Truth is the Holy Spirit.

1. Reproves the world of sin, righteousness, and of judgment.
2. Of sin because they believe not on me.
3. Of righteousness, because I go to my Father, and ye sse me no more.
4. Of judgment, because the prince of this world is judged.

The bible states that all lyers will have their part in the lake of fire. We need to be careful about putting under subjection a lying thought. Some people lie out of fear while others may lie to make themselves look important. Lying is not of God and should be avoided at all times.

CHAPTER 9

Familiar Spirit
The Spirit Of God

> _Lev. 20:6 And the soul that turns after such as familiar_
> _spirits and after wizards to go a whoring after them, I_
> _will even set my face against that soul and will cut him off_
> _among his people._

> _Deut. 18:11 Or a charmer or a consulter or a necromances._
> _Workers with familiar spirits and the wizards and the_
> _images and the idols and the abominat._

> _1Chron. 10:13 As king counsel of one that had a familiar_
> _spirit to enquire of it._
> _2Chron. 33:_

Roots are sorcery, witchcraft, astrology, fortune telling, tarrot cards, palm reading, idolatry, magicians and soothsayers.

In Leviticus it says regard not them that have familiar spirits. We are to be led by the Spirit of God.

I know many people who have their palms and cards read. Before I knew better, I would read the horoscope every day. If it said that I was going to have a bad day then guess what, I had a bad day. I found myself led by the things it would say because I believed what it would say. On the night that I gave my heart to Jesus the minister who prayed with me looked at me and said "God said stop dabbing around with horoscopes and things that have not been ordained by me. I created you and knew you before you were in the womb of your Mother. God has a plan for my life and I would not want to place my life in the hands of anyone but God. I do not want to listen to what any other false teaching or false doctrine has to say. I do not need to hear what confusious has to say. I can get confused enough on my own.

CHAPTER 10

Haughtiness Humble As A Butterfly

Roots that lead to a spirit of haughtiness or a haughty spirit are pride, proud look, puffed up, overbearing, arragance, unteachable spirit, dominating and controlling.

A haughty spirit wants to be in control at all times. It wants to keep people in the dark so that it is the only one that knows what is going on. Having it's own agenda, it will allow a few people to come into the click. It uses people and control situations to carry out the plan of the enemy. A haughty spirit wants to crush a humble spirit and suppress it to keep it down so that it can not do the work that God has called it to do and not be able to carry the plan out that the Lord has given it. It tries to dominate and control every situation. Its soul purpose is to get the glory, to take the credit of others who have worked hard into starting up or operating a ministry or just simply to claim ownership and title of something great that someone else did.

God places in the righteous, the gift of discernment. He has given his body special gifts and one of them is the gift of discernment. Not every one has this gift and others may have other special gifts such as gift of prophecy, that is the messenger to carry out the word of God. The gift of tongues whereas we are able to speak with heavenly tongues that only the Spirit of God knows. The interpretation of tongues which is someone who can interpret what the gift of tongues is speaking in their own language so that other people can know what the Spirit of God is saying. There are other gifts that God has given to men. It is Gods choice who has what gift and how many. One can discern by the gift of discernment. When discerning this haughty spirit the body can experience actual symptoms like not being able to take a deep breath. Usually a sharp pain in the back of the neck is a sure sign that a haughty spirit is around. Praying in the Holy Ghost releases the Spirit of God to trample down the haughty spirit and what so ever we bind on earth is bound by the Father in heaven. We loosen humbleness, submissiveness, gentleness and meekness.

God does not want his people to be in bondage to the haughty spirit nor does he want us to be under subjection to the haughty spirit. Haughty eyes, a proud heart and evil actions are all sin. In proverbs God hates seven things. Haughty eyes, a lying tongue, hands that kill the innocent, a heart that plots evil, feet that race to do wrong, a false witness who pours out lies and a person who sows discard in a family.

We are not here to control another human being nor to be put on a pedestal or to be put on our own throne. Jesus left his throne in heaven and became a servant on this earth and an example for us to follow. He continued to hate pride and arrogance and taught them that it was wrong but lived a meek and lowly life, humble and submissive, an example for us to live. A humble person can easily discern a haughty person but it is very important not to be suppressed by that person. Rise up above the haughtiness and take control. Refuse to be dominated or controlled by another person. No person should be in bondage and controlled by another. God has given us freedom and we are to walk in that freedom.

Pride means high or inordinate opinion of one's own dignity, importance, merit or superiority, whether as cherished in the mind or as displayed in bearing, conduct self esteem conceit.

Arragance means an offensive display of superiority or self importence, overbearing, pride.

Overbearing is domineering in manner, overwhelming in power or dictorial, haughtily or rudely arragent.

The opposite of a haughty spirit is a humble Spirit.

God loves a Humble Spirit and hate haughtiness. There are many men that carry a haughty spirit. God has placed in the heart of a man a protective gift so that he is able to take care of his family. Sometimes that gift is abused and protective ways turn into dominating and controlling ways.

Some women have also been known to carry this haughty spirit. Many divorces are caused because of this spirit.

It is very hard to function when you are attacked by this spirit. It may cause a person to loose their identity when they are dominated by another. They feel that they no longer have a mind of their own and someone else has all control of the decisions of their lives. This spirit can cause a person to have a week mind and to loose control of their total being.

Only God can deliver you from this spirit. Keep in mind life is not all about finding yourself but it is about discovering who God created you to be. We will never really know our true identity until we find our calling from God. Our identity is in Christ. Get out from this haughty spirit by humbling yourself unto the mighty hands of God and let God exalt you, deliver and strengthen your mind. Prayer can break the control of this spirit off of you. When we change our hearts and our minds then we become humble. God hates a haughty spirit but loves the humble.

CHAPTER 11

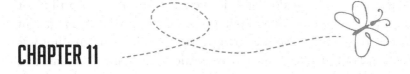

Heaviness Inside Of The Cocoon

> *Isaiah. 61:3 To Appoint unto them that mourn unto Zion,*
> *to give unto them beauty for ashes, the oil for mourning, the*
> *garment of praise for the spirit of heaviness that they might*
> *be called trees of righteousness the planting of the Lord that*
> *he might be glorified.*

The definition for heaviness is feeble, absure, somewhat dark, darkish, was dim, to be sick, distress, sad, mourning, lamentations, depression, affliction, distress (mind). Does some of these sound familiar to you. Have you ever felt like you were in a deep pit and could not climb out.

Some of the roots are a wounded spirit, mourning, sorrow, grief, depression, heavy laden and heavy burden. Before I accepted the Lord as my savior I remember being so depressed that I could not get out of bed to send my children off to school. I remember thinking I wanted to live but on the inside I was dead. Darkness had consumed me. After years of abuse, neglect, hurts, scars and wounds death had taken hold of me. The decease grip would not let me go. I felt it on the inside as well as on the out and I was not able to do anything about it. I set up an appointment for me at a psychiatric clinic on a Wednesday after I realized that I was not able to shake this on my own. On the Tuesday night before the appointment, I attended a women's meeting. On February 18, 1992 around 8:00 that night I confessed Jesus as my Lord and Savior. Since that night the Lord started to take layers of all the hurt and pain and removed it far from me. That night was the last night that I put a cigarette in my mouth. Instantaneously, I was delivered from smoking. Only God can do that. He brought me out of a horrible pit and set my feet upon a rock and put a new song in my heart. He taught my hands to war. He gave me strength and joy. The old creature was dead and out of the ashes came a new creation full of life. I became as a butterfly and I loved life again. God gave me my identity. I found loving the little things again like singing and dancing, butterflies and smiling faces, children and horses. I realized I had gifts in me that I never knew I had. I was no longer just Mrs. Michael Bradford but I was Annie again with more of the vibrant life that I had ever imagined that I could have. God gave me back the years that the canker worm stole from me. The enemy, the devil himself robbed me but with God all things are possible. We must believe and not walk after the flesh but after the Spirit of God. Today I do not know where God is leading and guiding me but I do know that he is in control of my life. I learned to just let go and let God. My life was more precious and valuable when I gave it to him than when I was trying to run it my own way.

Almost seventeen years later in 2007 that same heaviness that gripped me before was trying to creep back into my life once again. That dull moth of a life that was wasting away and seemingly had no meaning tried to consume me again when we received a tragic phone call from our son that our grandson had went to be with Jesus in his sleep. The enemy knew the one thing that could break me and send me back into that pit was the harm of my children or grandchildren. I soon found myself battling that same stronghold again. Yes we win battles but the war never ends. We know what side will win. With all courage and the strength of God in me Jesus kept my feet from falling once again. God turned a horrible situation into a ministry. We now help pay for headstones and some burial expenses for parents who have loss their children up to ten years old. A healing came as our compassion helped to heal others arose. What was meant for evil God turned it around for good. We have hope and anticipation that one day we will be with our grandson again along with all of our relatives who went on before us.

Condemnation can sometimes cause depression. Many times as a child we have done something to make us guilty or condemned. When we are older we carry that weight around. Lester Summerall speaks in one of his syllabus that condemnation is in our soulish part of our being. A guilty feeling is a feeling when you have done something wrong marally. A doing that causes condemnation. An open door to condemnation is a covered sin. Book of Proverb says "One who covers sin shall not prosper". We must confess and forsake sin. The enemy loves to throw our past back at us. A soft answer is yes but I have been forgiven devil. Did you ask for forgiveness? Two men were hung side by side of Jesus on that Friday that he was killed for all mankind. The only difference between one from the other was that one repented and the other did not. Jesus said to the thief on the cross when he asked for repentence "This day you shall be with me in paradise. The thief had a lot of guilty sin that he needed repenting about. His guilt led him to repentence. His sin led him to Jesus. When we repent sin is cast into the lake of fire. There is no reason why we should live twenty years with guilt and shame inside of us when we have forgiveness if we ask for it. Depression grows when we do not cast that guilt or shame out of us.

Luke 22:62 states that Peter wept bitterly when he denied Christ three times. Peter went into repentence at what he had done in denying Jesus. Judas on the other hand betrayed Jesus and went and hung himself. The guilt and shame that he had done to Jesus destroyed him. Judas had all power to repent and ask Jesus to forgive him but his selfish pride would not let him. God would have been faithful and just to forgive him of all his sins and to cleanse him from all of his unrighteousness.

The prodical son went through a prideful time. His choice landed him eating with the pigs. When he came home and asked his Father for forgiveness his father gave him a huge welcome home party.

He was forgiven by his Father and was free from the dark pit that he had dug himself into. We always have a way out but it is our choice to take it. Nothing is hopeless but the enemy tries to get us to believe that there is no way out. The deeper we get into depression the harder it is for us to come out of it. A weak mind is easily attacked and can trigger suicidal or homocidal thoughts. Noticing these triggers and dealing with these thoughts early can prevent a spirit of heaviness to come upon you. It is very hard but not impossible to come out of that dark place on your own. Crying out to Jesus can release and break that hold that the enemy has on you. Jesus strengthens your mind and causes you to be complete and full of God. He pours the oil of gladness upon your head for the spirit of heaviness. With all of your strength get up and put on praise and worship music. This breaks the yokes of bondages that the enemy has upon you. This releases a joyful Godly spirit in the atmosphere.

There are many times that the spirit of heaviness tries to come back on me. As long as we allow these things to attach itself to our minds and thoughts we are most vulnerable to it. When life takes a turn in another direction and you experience a change in your life you should be prepared to experience this spirit again.

My husband and I had been working together in the ministry for what was going on the sixth year. The drug war and violence in Mexico became so bad that we were forced not to go back into the border towns. We had been warned three times in one day not to go back into Mexico. The drug cortels had been shooting from Mexico to across the Rio Grande River into the United States. Missionaries were getting shot. On one particular day the drug cortels tried to steal a truck while a Missionary and his wife were in it. When they tried to escape they shot at the truck and the passenger, the Missionarie's wife was shot in the head. Renosa Mexico, the city where the clinic and the children's feeding station had been feeling the brunt of the war.

We had to make the decision to go back to work for awhile. Our contrubutions and support had been cut out from the churches. Mike was hired on to go back into the oilfield. He found himself going offshore again. A job that neither one of us ever expected. Mike never wanted to go back into the oilfield. He had been in the oilfield many years ago. Although there is plenty of money to be made in the oilfield we have to trade one of the most precious gifts from God, our time. They say when we have money we have no time and when we have time we have no money. This saying became alive to us again. We prayed for a balance in both so that we can be able to continue doing the work of the ministry. Mike's heart was to continue to financially support some of the ministers that we had been supporting. Our Missionary friends needed supplies and funding. We also wanted to help out the girls in Vera Cruz. They had been such a blessing and God was using them mightlily. We needed to continue over twenty five projects that was started by our own ministry. This would be one more great sacrifice that we would have to endure. We would be financially set to accomplish all of our goals in the coming years. People were counting on us such as poor project neighborhoods for school uniforms, school supplies, Christmas presents, blankets, pillows, food and supplies to the homeless. God opened the door for a great oilfield company to hire Mike. I would continue the work of the ministry and work with children. When Mike was in we would make our trips to the border of Mexico to bring the long awaited supplies for the Missionaries, Pastors and the people along the border. We would also be able to continue to support our Pastor and friend in Guyana, South America.

Seperation anxiety did not take long to expose itself in me. I would soon feel the strongest and greatest sacrifice of all that would hit me, lonliness. Lonliness was driving me crazy eventhough I had more work than time. Amazing all of the emotions that you go through when there is one change in our every day life. In one week I was hit with fear, heaviness and many other strongholds that tried to creep into the weakness of my own thoughts and mind. One more season for the enemy to attack. The thief cometh not but to steal, kill and destroy. Thank God Jesus came to bring life and life more abundantly. Thank God that he worked overtime in that week for me. Although I was getting bombarded with many strongholds that tried to destroy me, amazingly, God was holding all of them back. My holding on to the true word of God and my faith in him saved me once again from this destructive stronghold.

Life has many disappointments. Disappointments is a feeling of being let down. A feeling of sadness or frustration because something

49

was not as good, attractive or satisfactory as expected or because something that we hope for did not happen. Frustration is defined as the failure to attain hopes and wishes. I can remember many times of feeling these emotions. When my children were making decisions that were not in their best interest. We all must make our own decisions but we all must also live with the decisions and consequences of our choices. Bad things have followed us as a result of our choices. These results can cause great sorrow for the family and everyone involved. Can you recall a decision that you made in your life that caused great sorrow for every one involved. I know I made decisions that affected the lives of others. We try to do what is best at all times but our choices do have consequences whether they are good or bad. Almost all of our bad choices come from our inmaturity or out of pure ignorance. Some may have been caused by a rebellious spirit or some by acting spontaneously. We need to remember that our choices does not affect only us but every one involved. If we pause for a moment and think about the decision we are about to make and conclude the best choice to make then we will make the best decision for ourselves as well as every one involved. If we ask ourselves questions before we make the final decision than we can usually make the right decision. For example if you are feeling so much rage to the point where it is uncontrollable. Stop before you decide to harm or even murder another person and ask youself do I want to spend the rest of my life in prison or do I want to get the death penalty. I am sure we all can agree that any logical person in their right mind would choose not to murder. It is very important that we decide to choose the right thing before we get into a position where we are out of control. Knowing what to do and being prepared to do the right thing causes us to ultimately make the righ decision should it arise. Prayer before making an important decision is the best key. God helps us with wisdom and understanding. We should never be guided by our own desires but we should yield ourselves to what is best for us in the eyes of God.

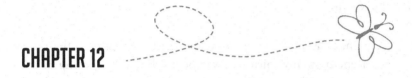

CHAPTER 12

Bondage
Butterfly Transformation

The butterfly life cycle consist of the egg, the larva which is the caterpillar, the pupa (chrysalis) and the butterfly. The pupa stage in most butterflies is one which there is very little movement. When the caterpillar is completely grown it forms a protective shield called pupa. This is where the transformation from a caterpillar to a butterfly takes place. When the pupa has finished transformation the butterfly emerges from the pupa.

When there is very little movement in our lives is when God is transforming us from living in the flesh to living in his Spirit. We must allow God to transform us into his Spirit.

If we live after the flesh we will die but if we through the spirit of God mortify the deeds of the body we will live. For as many as are led by the Spirit of God they are the sons of God. For we have not received the spirit of bondages again to fear but we have received the Spirit of adoption whereby we cry Abba Father.

The definition of bondage is to tread down, to disregard, to conquer, violate, force, keep under, subdue, bring into subjection, enslave, serve, make servant, transgress, slavery.

The roots of bondage are abundance and excessive wine, excessive drinking, overeating, laziness, constant gambling, smoking, habitual drunkenness, reveling and winebibbers. Our flesh love the things that harm us. Our flesh is enemies to God and his works. We have to put our flesh into subjection to the word of God. We are not able to fight spiritual battles with our flesh. Practicing self control daily is one way to subject our flesh. We can not control the spirit of bondage without God's help.

I remember about twent years ago when I first came to the Lord and was experiencing many spiritual awareness. Mike was working in the oilfield with a shop full of smokers. One day I was crying out to Lord on the floor and I seen in my spirit all the people at the shop smoking. I began to intercede for them one by one. Amazingly the next couple of weeks they had all began to stop smoking. Deliverance came in and it was such a surprise to see God move in the mist of the spirit of bondage. He broke the chains of darkness that had attached itself and released the people from that bondage. A spirit of bondage has more of a chance at being bound up than the works of the flesh. Your flesh can decide to smoke if it wants to and it can decide to stop if it does not want to. Any spirit can be bound and loosen because the flesh has a God given choice but an evil spirit has no choice. God has given us all power and authority to break it. If we choose to allow and we love our flesh to smoke, gamble or drink in excess than it is not a spirit. Therefore it is much harder to heal a person to whom their flesh has given authority to the enemy.

CHAPTER 13

Perverse Spirit
Wounded Wings

A wounded Spirit shows signs of hurt, injured, offended, insulted, affronted, upset and snubbed out. These wounded injuries embed deep into our hearts causing a stronghold, the perverse spirit. If we continue to allow these wounds to affect our spirit the perverted spirit seed grows and produces roots. Some of these roots that contain this stronghold are incest, homosexuals, sodomites and rapists, evil actions caused by immoral events that was done to you or done by you, these constant malevolence proceedings become rooted and grounded and deep within our soul and causes us to either be bitter or better whichever one we allow to pursue.

We must not fool ourselves into thinking that our ways are always the right ways. The bible says there is a way that seems right unto man but the end result is death. We fall into doctrinal or physical error, inaccuracy, miscalculation and incorrectness. Our mind becomes incomplete and sort of speaking, wired wrong. Foolish, silly, idiotic, unwise and imprudent thinking. Therefore creating debatable conversations, contentious arguments, disagreements, conflicts and controversies leading to contention and strife.

An incomplete mind produces a chronic worrier with persistent frets and continual bothers. Our minds can not be turned off and the reality is that peace have left us and we are no longer complete in God who is the head of all powers, principalities, rulers and spiritual wickedness in high places. Our brain becomes dirty with smutty intelligence, a mucky mentality and a filthy mind that thinks only distorted things such as sexual perversion, distorted sexual characteristics, twisting of sexual category, incest thinking and carrying out of different abuses. Our mind is the first home of a thought soon dropping into our hearts and finally out of our mouths by speaking or acting upon it and by living it out. If we put our mind and thoughts into subjection we can stop it before it gets out of control. We need to destroy the bad thoughts and destroy if before it becomes a seed that takes root. We are supposed to meditate on what is good, and what is the perfect will of God.

CHAPTER 14

Other Strongholds
Flightless

On a windy Summer morning in the Rio Grande Valley, I had been cleaning the place that we called home. We stayed in a 5th wheeler that was given to us after we had purchased an RV from Missionary friends for 1,500 dollars. I was so happy because it meant that I had a full size bath and a full size bed. After sweeping my mat outside that morning I noticed a beautiful single butterfly that had somehow been wounded. It was not able to fly. I could not find it in my heart to leave him there. I took him inside and made him a house with grass in a little bowl. Even though I have seen millions of butterflies come to the valley and stop in for rest before their long journey of migration to South America, I felt the urgency to save this particular colorful butterfly. It's wings were wounded and needed someone to help. Just as it needed someone to help we also have needs. Our wings can at times be broken and we are not able to get off the ground. I took care of the butterfly until it was strong enough to be placed outside where he then flew off. God takes care of his children when we are not able to spread our wings and fly. They that wait upon the Lord will renew their strength. They will run and not be weary. They will walk and not faint.

anti-Christ spirit 1John 4:3
Every spirit that confesses not that Jesus Christ is come in the flesh is not of God, and this spirit is that spirit of anti-Christ.

Roots: (Definitions)
False Witnesses—Mth. 24:4-5, 1Cor. 14:29
False—Not according with truth or fact. Incorrect. Not according with rules or law.
A person who did not see an event, crime or accident take place but claims to be eye witness.
False evidence, false testimony, false proof.
Someone who speaks against Christ. Someone who confesses not Christ is an athiest.
Similar to a lying spirit but speaks against Christ.
Spiritual spirit that is against Christ.
Doesn't acknowledge that Jesus is Lord and Savior to all. Lord of heaven and earth. The Savior of all the world.
Synonyms: counterfeit, phoney, bogus, untrue.
False Prophet—Mth. 7:15—Someone who speaks not with the Spirit of God but with the enemy or flesh.
Error—1John 4:6, John 15, 26
Error—A mistake, the state or condition of being wrong in conduct or judgment. A Belief that unintentionally deviates from what is correct, right or true. Deviation from accuracy or correctness. a mistake, as in action or speech.
Synonyms
mistake, fault, lapse, slip, blunder

Mammon Spirit has many roots.
One is a root of greed. A desire to acquire wealth beyond what one needs to consume it upon our own flesh. Covetousness is a strong desire of another persons property and God warns us of this in the ten commandments. Materialistic is another root leading to the mammon spirit. A strong desire of things that have us instead of us having these things. Desiring more of the world is another root leading to this spirit. 1Timothy chapter 6 states that for the love of

money is the root of all evil which while some coveted after they have erred from faith and pierced themselves through with many sorrows. Money is not the root of all evil. The love (lust) of money is the root of all evil. Using money to consume it upon our own fleshly desires can destroy us and our relationship with Jesus.

Judas betrayed Jesus and his innocent blood for thirty peaces of silver. Judas allowed the lust of money that eventually destroyed him.

Creating Success from running our own business is to remember that we are able to give back to our community. Our success has to come when we give. When we seek first the kingdom of God and his righteousness every thing will be added onto us. If we choose to hold back and spend it all upon ourselves we deprive the blessings from coming in. The principle of giving works. When we give it will be given onto us. Our financial responsibilities and duties are laid out for us and is written by God in the bible. We should use our financial resources for the gospel, the less fortunate and the needy. We should remember that our financial blessings is a gift from God. We are to be wise at all times in using our income to be a blessing and not a curse towards others. Turning these blessings over for good and not for evil.

We should never let prosperity turn our hearts away from God. Ask ourselves are we doing good with our finances? Providing for our families with the basic needs such as food, shelter and clothing. Are we providing for the needy, homeless and orphans in and out of our community. Are we expanding the gospel as we should be doing.

Our qualifications which is our talents that God has equipped each of us with causes us to have great earnings and wealth. God has given us gifts inside of us. Your gift is different from mine yet we all work together in disbursing our gifts to contribute to the world in making it a better place to live. One may be a Teacher and another may be a Doctor. We are all important and every one does have special gifts and qualities that make us who we are. We may have many gifts also that we are able to do many good works that cause us to accumulate great wealth. All gifts and talents come from God that allows us to get great earnings and wealth.

Proverbs 13:22 it states "A good man attempts to leave an inheritence for his childrens children where as the wealth of wicked is laid up for the righteous. A wise wealthy man will leave an inheritance but a fool will spend his money unwisely and will not have any left. A giving Spirit should take the place of a mammon spirit.

Doubt and Unbelief Spirit

Roots that lead to a doubt and unbelief spirit are apostasy-(christianity) rejection of christianity by someone who formerly was a christian.

Turning away from, liberalism-lacking moral restraint, favoring, based upon principles of liberalism.

Moderism-practice, usage, expression perculiar to modern times, tendency in theology to accommodte traditional religious teaching to contemporary thought and especially to devalue supernatural elements, self councious break with the past and a search for new forms of expressions.

syncretism-combination of different forms of belief or practice. disbelief, falsehood, godlessness, impenitence and infidelity.

And immediately Jesus stretched forth his hand and caught him and said unto him, "Oh thou of little faith, wherefore didst thou doubt.

If we choose to have doubt and unbelief we can not enter the kingdom of God.

Faith is the opposite of doubt and unbelief.

An atheist spirit which is a disbelieving, agnostic, doubting and skeptical spirit can arise from the depth of our souls when we shut down and choose to quit believing or never did believe in any one such as God, Jesus or the Holy Spirit or in any thing. However an atheist admits that they do not have faith in anything whereas they choose to believe not to believe. If you think about it for just a moment you can see that every one believes in something whether an atheist chooses to believe that there is no God. They truly believe therefore they believe in something. That there is no God.

Well if you are going to use your strength or effort in believing that there is no God then we just as well believe that there is a God.

This way if your belief is that there is no

God and there is no God you have gained nothing. But if your belief is that there is no God and there is a God then you have gained eternal hell. Keep in mind just because you do not believe something it does not mean that it is not there. We choose to believe things and not believe things but it does not mean that we are right in our own beliefs.

Seducing spirit

To lead astray, to wander, to delude, deceive, beguile, entice, persuade, provoke, remove, take away, to err, make to stagger, cause to wander. In Timothy the Spirit speaks expressly that in the latter times some shall depart from the faith giving heed to seducing spirits and doctrines of devils. Some of the roots are speaking lies, forbidding to marry, abstaining from meats, alluring away from truth and false teachers. A seducing spirit can persuade a person into another direction. Sadly we can lead someone away from what God has for them. They mind can go from complete to doubleminded. A person who thrives for their own way is susceptible to this spirit. The devil beguiled Eve in the garden of Eden. He seduced her by telling her a lie. By deceiving her, she and Adam disobeyed what God told them to do. God said that in the latter days some shall depart from the faith giving heed to seducing spirits and doctrines of devils. The very elect shall be deceived. We have to be careful not to be seduced into doing things that our flesh will have a hard time overcoming.

CHAPTER 15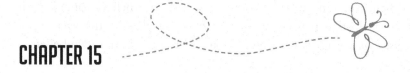

Taking To Flight

While working in the ministry in the valley down in the Rio Grande, I had an awesome privilege to see an assortment of beautiful butterflies. I love to sit and observe them. Their sensitivity as they land on the ground. Some of them thrive with great trouble to go from the ground to take flight. Butterflies are so fragile yet they can travel thousands of miles. They stop in at the valley for a rest before they continue their great flight into South America. The strong's survive and the weak ones journey sadly ends in the valley.

In the same description of the sensitive and delicate wings of a butterfly so are the spiritual gifts that God provides for us. His nine spiritual gifts are for us to use for the body of Christ to be equipped and complete in him. If you are not aware of the bible and what God has for his children you will live your life and never experience the pure and natural gifts of the Spirit of God.

One of his gifts is discernment. The gift of discernment is a protective discerning to feel or know, good or bad and what will happen before it happens. Physical or spiritual danger warning signs that the Lord shows you before it comes. It can also detect evil spirits before it does any damage. Sort of a spiritual antenna placed on our heads.

An example of physical discernment is when you or walking or someone you know walks outside and there is a busy intersection or highway and you look both ways before you cross it. Your eyes are your physical discernment protecting you or someone you know from the harm that can come to you. The same with your spiritual eyes. You can look in the front, back and on both sides to protect you from getting hurt. This is one of the gifts that God has left for us on this earth. We do not have to be in the dark if we are using discernment.

Discernment is one of the nine gifts that God gave us. Another gift is wisdom. The gift of wisdom stops us when our mind and thoughts are not right. Wisdom is knowledge and insight perception. Wisdom teaches us to use good judgment and is intelligent. It gives us understanding and places us on the right path and keeps us there. When God created the heavens and the earth wisdom was there.

The armor is a spiritual protection that God has given us. For we wrestle not against flesh and blood but against powers, rulers and principalities and spiritual wickedness in high places.

When you are a child of God the bible says that your are protected by a supernatural armor. It is invisible and you can not see it or feel it. We are told to put on the whole armor of God in order to protect ourselves from satins powers and influences and his schemes.

Here is a poem that I wrote about a battle between our flesh and our spirit is always warring.

The Battle
Call it a war or call it a fight
But the battle still begins tonight
Arm and arm we are ready for flight
It starts now. It is not a pretty sight
Men we say are very bold

61

Honor runs down as precious gold
There goes one. There goes two
We really don't know what we are getting into
It starts to thunder, lightening and rain
I can sense honor, love but above all the pain
But there is sense of pride in every man
A feeling that only God can understand
For what does it gain a man to loose his own soul
Never blaming himself and all the things he can not control
You can call it a war or you can call it a fight
But the battle of our soul begins morning, noon and night
So get on that armor, get ready, Let's Fight

Where To Find Help When dealing with these roots. Refer to these scriptures to get you though the rough times.

Afraid—Psalms 34:4, Mathew 10:28, 11Timothy1:7, Hebrew13:5, 6
Anxious—Psalm 46, Mathew 6:19-34, Phil. 4:6, 1 Peter 5:6
Backsliding—Psalm 51, 1John 1:4-9
Bitter or Critical—1Cor. 13
Defeated—Romans 8:31-39
Depressed—Psalm 34
Disaster Threatens—Psalm 91, Psalm 118:5-6, Luke 8:22-25
Discouraged—Psalm 23:42—
Doubting—Mathew 8:26/Heb. 11
Facing A Crisis—Psalm 121/Mathew 6:25-34/Heb. 4:16
Faith Fails—Psalm 42:5/Heb. 11
Friends Fail—Psalm 41:9-13/Luke 17:3-4/Romans 12:14, 17, 19, 21/11Timothy 4:16-18
Leaving Home—Psalm 121/Mathew 10:16-20
Lonely—Psalm 23/Heb. 13:5, 6
Needing God's Protection—Psalm 27:1-6, 91/Phil. 4:19
Needing Guidance—Psalm 32:8/Proverb 3:5, 6
Needing Peace—John 14:1-4, 16:33/Romans 5:1-5/Phil. 4:6, 7
Needing Rules for Living: Romans 12
Overcome—Psalm 6/Romans 8:31-39/1John 1:4-9

Prayerful—Psalm4/Psalm 42/Luke 11:1-13/John 17/1Josh 5:14, 15

Protected—Psalm 18:1-3, 34:7

Sick or in Pain—Psalm 38/Mathew 26:39/ romans 5:3-5 11Cor. 12:9, 10/ 1Peter 4:12, 13, 19

Sorrowful—Psalm 51/Mathew 5:4/ John 14/11Cor. 1:3, 4/ 1 Thes. 4:13-18

Tempted—Psalm 1: 139:23, 24/ Mathew 26:41/ 1Cor. 10:12-14/ Phil. 4:8/ James 4:7/ 11Peter 2:9, 3:17

Thankful—Psalm 100/ 1Thes. 5:18/ Heb. 13:15

Traveling—Psalm 121

Trouble, In—Psalm 16/ Psalm 31/ John 14:1-4/ Heb. 7:25

Weary—Psalm 90/ Mathew 11:28-30/ 1Cor. 15:58/ Gal. 6:9, 10

Worried—Mathew 6:19-34/ 1Peter 5:6, 7

Adultery: Mathew 5:27-32

Adversity: Mathew 10:16-39

Anger: Mathew 5:22-24

Anxiety: Mathew 6:19-24

Conceit: Luke 18:9-14

Confidence: False: Mathew 7:24-27

Covetousness: Mark 7:21-23

Crime: Mathew 15:17-20

Death: John 11:25, 26

Deceit: Mathew 23:27, 28

Depravity: John 3:19-21

Divorce: Mark 10:2-12

Doubt: Mathew 14:28-31

Drunkenness: Luke 21:34-36

Enemies: Mathew 5:43-48

Excuses: Luke 14:15-24

Extravangance: 1Timothy 6:7-12

Falsehood: Rev. 21:8

Faultfinding: Mathew 7:1-5

Fear: Luke 12:5

Flesh: Rom. 13:14

Greed: Luke 12:15-31

Hatred: Mathew 5:43-48

Intemperance: Proverb 20:1

Judging: Mathew 7:1
Lip-Service: Mathew 7:21
Lust: Mark 4:18, 19
Pride: 1John 2:15-17
Revenge: Mathew 5:43-48
Self-Exultation: Luke 14:11
Self-Righteousness: Luke 18:11, 12
Sin: John 8:34-36
Submission: 1Peter 2:13-17
Swearing: Colos. 3:8
Temptation: 1Cor. 10:13
Tribulation: John 16:33
Worldliness: 1John 2:15-17

Other Study Scriptures:

Mathew 18:18—Bind and Loosen
Ephes. 6:10-17 Armor of God
Galat. 5:22-25 Fruit of Spirit Of God
Mathew 16:19, John 20:23
Doubt And Unbelief Spirit
Mathew 21:21, John 10:24-27, Mark 9:24, 2Corin. 6:14, Mathew 14:31,

CHAPTER 16

Closing Metamorphoses, New Creation

Metamorphoses is the name for rapid transfornation of a larva into an adult that occur in some insects. The caterpilla transforms into a butterfly. The butterfly becomes a new creation as it emerges from the pupa. The adult butterfly lays eggs on plants after the mating period and the process starts all over again from the eggs to the larva stage to the pupa and the butterfly. The beautiful monarch butterfly always choose a safe place to lay the eggs. The eggs are safe from harm underneath a leaf.

God has a safe place for us to dwell in. The secret place of the most high. He spreads his wings and cover us with his feathers and we dwell safely in him. Our spirits soar as eagles when we are tucked away in him. When we walk in his Spirit and have the mind and thoughts of him we shall not fulfill the lust of the flesh. When are we walking in the flesh? When we have fleshly thoughts contrary to God.

When did the seed thought get in you?

The seed of jealousy took root when I had just gotten married to Mike and we were not living a righteous life. I no longer trusted Mike when he would walk out of the door because he gave me reason not to just as I began to give him reason not to trust me also. I held on to the insecurities that created jealousy. My suspicions and distrusts had taken root and created the seed of jealousy. The stronghold stayed with me until the Lord showed me how to get rid of it. By living totally opposite of envy I gained my confidence in the Lord. I trusted in God that he would take care of all my insecurties. He would remove all of my timid feelings. He turned jealousy into confidence. I soon realized that man can not be trusted and never will be able to be trusted because flesh is enemies to God and our own selves. Our flesh wants to destroy us because it lives to please ourselves. God wants us to live to please others. This can be very complicated, demanding and challenging. When you live to please others self is under subjection, self is disciplined and controlled.

The only way that we can deal with the emotions of our flesh is by the word of God and his Spiritual gifts. God does not want us to be ignorant of the gifts of the Spirit through the Holy Ghost. There are different administrations or ministries but we have one God. There are different operations or activities but the same God works in all of them. The manifestation of the gifts are given to us to profit all. There are nine gifts of the spirit. They include word of wisdom, word of knowledge, faith, gift of healing, working of miracles, prophecy, discerning of spirits, divers kinds of tonguesand the interpretation of tongues. These gifts are very important for the body to become one in Christ. Now whether we be Jews or Gentiles, bond or free, we are all made into one Spirit. The whole body has many members within the body yet one Spirit. So the foot can not say to the hand "You are not the body" or the ear can not say "because you are not the eye you are not the body". The whole body can not be the eye because how would the body hear or smell. But God set the members in the body as it pleases him. There are many members yet one body. Which leads us into the members of the body that God has set in the church today as the five fold ministry, Apostles, Prophets, Teachers, Pastors and Evangelists. Other members include miracles, gifts of healings, helps and governments and diversities of tongues. These members of one body make up what we call "The Church" today.

We can sit around, dream and wonder what is our purpose in life? Who are we really? Where are we going or what are we really doing in life? What is our reason and place in this world? The truth is that only God can give us our clear identity and our clear direction and guidance. In God we can blossom into who he wants us to be. Our new creation is in him.

And now let us begin our journey chasing after the one true genuine monarch. We have been taught the roots and signs of strongholds that weigh us down. We have been led in the ways that we should go. We have learned that all we really ever had to be is who and what God created us to be. He has ordained us since before the world began and he knows our identity. Confusion comes in when we add all of our earthly desires. When we choose all of our fleshly passions. My need to be successful in life was driving me into other directions. My desire to be important placed me on other paths in life. Ultimately all of my success stories ended up in failure. In the past the store that I had been managing for five years and was number one in sales each week somehow was forced to close it's doors. As hard as I worked at being number one, the destiny of the store was not in my hands. The parent company went bankrupt. It was in God's hands. All of my hard work had somehow ended in vain. I packed up the store and we said all of our sad goodbye's and locked the door for the last time. That chapter of the book called "My Life" was over and I could not control it on my own nor could I ever get it back.

Solomon as claimed in Ecclesiastes is the wisest, richest and most influential king in Israel's history. He looks at life under the sun and from a human perspective. He declares it to be all empty. Power, popularity, prestige and pleasure. Nothing can fill the void in man's life but God himself. But when we see it from God's perspective, life takes on a whole new meaning and purpose causing Solomon to exclaim, "EAT . . . DRINK . . . REJOICE . . . DO GOOD . . . LIVE JOYFULLY . . . FEAR GOD . . . KEEP HIS COMMANDMENTS!"

In Ecclesiates Solomon stresses that all is vanity. The illustrations of vanity includes one generation passes away and another generation comes. The sun rises and the sun goes down and is eager for his place where he arose. The wind goes toward the south and turns about unto the north. It whirls about continually and the wind returns again. All the rivers run into the sea and yet the sea is not full. Where the rivers come is where they return again. All things are wearisome of labor and man can not express it. The eye is not satisfied with seeing nor the ear filled with hearing. The thing that has been it is that which shall be. That which is done is that which shall be done and there is no new thing under the sun. All is in vain. The vanity of striving after earthly wisdom. The vanity of striving after pleasure. The vanity of striving for great accomplishments. The vanity of hard labour. Now do not misinterpret me by giving up on life and not striving for excellence. What God is saying that it will all one day pass away and be of no existence. As long as we are living on earth we must have wealth to function. The world thrives on wealth but we must strive to be content. God predetermines the events of life. God predetermines the conditions of life. There is no suffficiency of wealth in heaven. Wealth comes ultimately from God and he owns everything. When all is said and done all we have to do is look forward to an eternal life with Christ.

We have to ask ourselves, Do we want to live life trying to be a genuine and colorful butterfly? Do we prefer to take life to unlimited and unboundless flight? Do we want to conquer and win battles. Or do we want to stay living as a dull, unexcited, motionless moth. One who is corrupted and waste away. One who's life experiences were eaten up by the canker worm and destroyed. Today we have that choice. Let us begin our incredible journey and limitless flight into a long process of finding our place in this world. Our own distinguished, illustrious thumb print on this earth. Our astonishing heart reaching, soul searching experiences that will ultimately lead us into an impressive, peaceful, tranquil, prosperous and successful life.

Life is not a remote control. Get up and turn it yourself.

Scriptures and other books used in the making of this book are from

King James Commentary Bible

King James NLT Bible

Webster Dictionary

If you read this book and would love to know more about Jesus and the love of God write to me or call faithministry07@yahoo.com 985-665-8476

Want to know more about our tax exempt, public charity? Need to order copies and other books? Check out our website www.faithministriesinternational.bellstrike.com

Other books written by Anna C. Bradford

At The Border by Anna C. Bradford

A Child's Journey by Anna C. Bradford

To order copies
985-665-8476
faithministry07@yahoo.com or
authorhouse.com/ChasingAfterButterflies/Anna C. Bradford
authorhouse.com/At The Border/Anna C. Bradford
Available at all major book stores. Kindle And Nook

About The Author

A Licensed Minister of the Gospel since 1999.

Background: Teacher and Director of Christian Academy Pre-School and Home School.

Owner and Director of Noah's Ark Pre-School and Learning Center.

Started up and Directed Living Jewels Pre-School and Learning Center.

Along side of her husband Mike, was called to full time ministry and Missionaries in 2007. Missionary presently to the United States, Mexico, South America, South Africa and Pakitstan.

Founders of Faith Ministries, International. A non profit, public charity organization to the poor and the needy children and their families. A multi culture, multi ministry.

Author and writer of *At The Border by Anna C. Bradford*, Childrens Lessons, Childrens Curriculum and Stories.